Section One

Section Two

Section Three

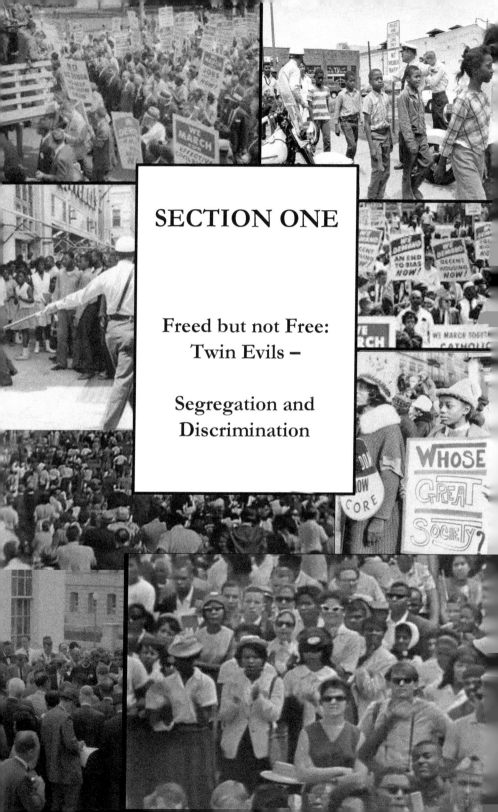

SECTION ONE

Freed but not Free:
Twin Evils –

Segregation and
Discrimination

In 1619, the first black slaves were brought to America and landed in Jamestown, Virginia. For 244 years, generation-after-generation of African Americans languished in an oppressive institution that wasn't abolished until January 1, 1863, when President Abraham Lincoln signed the Emancipation Proclamation, which extricated our forefathers and mothers from the shackles of slavery. Despite those actions; however, blacks would remain in some form of enslavement for years to come, and to this day they are not completely free of racism.

Freed slaves were not really free. They had to deal with the systemic octopus of racism that had its tentacles in every aspect of their lives. In 1860, Pittsylvania County had one of the largest slave populations in the state of Virginia, numbering 14,340 slaves. Ten years later, in 1870, the county had one of the largest African American populations in Virginia, with 16,084 blacks living in Danville. Fast forward one hundred years, after the signing of the Emancipation Proclamation, to 1963. Black people were still enslaved and confronted with the social fraternal twin demons, known as segregation and discrimination; fraternal, because there is a close association, but they are not exactly the same.

Segregation and discrimination are related because they are similar in their devastation and impact on the human spirit, but unlike identical twins, different. Each, however, was used to keep blacks from basic freedoms. In 1963 Danville schools operated under Plessy vs. Ferguson, a landmark decision of the United States Supreme Court in 1896 which upheld the constitutionality of racial segregation laws for public facilities as long as the facilities were equal in quality. This doctrine become known as "separate but equal". Thus, schools in Danville were homogeneously grouped.

Common signage in 1963

In Baltimore, Washington DC and Danville, people were protesting.

The system, at that time, was designed to prevent heterogeneous classrooms. All black students went to black schools and white students went to all-white schools. Neither group could sit in the same classrooms together, because segregationists were committed to keeping them apart. However, the truth of the matter was that schools were separate, but never equal.

Later, the Supreme Court decided in the case of Brown vs. the Board of Education in Topeka, Kansas, in 1954, that "separate but equal" was unconstitutional. We were living in *de facto* segregation, which meant it was segregation by fact though not by law. In the truest sense, segregation was designed to keep the races apart, and for decades after slavery, it did just that. In nearly all aspects of life, segregation was a massive form of oppression that kept the black community from equality in housing, schools, medical care and other basic necessities of life. So yes, we were free from physical bondage and living on a plantation, per se, but not freed from inferior treatment or status.

Discrimination is any action that takes race into account. In reference to employment requirements being met by both parties, if a business would rather hire a white person for the job rather than a black person, that would be discrimination. If a restaurant refused to serve black people, or even did what it could to discourage them from eating, that would be discrimination. It is not as systematic and "out front" as segregation. In a nutshell, segregation is what you do, while discrimination is what you think. It was an attempt to treat black people as *persona-non-grata* and to marginalize us.

Discrimination and segregation were rampant in Danville and in other cities around the nation, as blacks weren't allowed in numerous establishments or hired for positions for which they were fully qualified. Throughout my story, these twins will

The Jim Crow persona was a theater character by Thomas D. Rice and an ethnic depiction in accordance with contemporary white ideas of African Americans and their culture.

Above is one of the protesters making it plain that, **"Jim Crow must Go!"**

resonate as they have been a part of daily life for those in the black community.

From Birth to Death – Segregated Lives

For hundreds of years, white people saw the black man always coming through the back door of life, and they were seen as less than a white person. White people then, and even some now, have had an ethnocentric complex, believing that white people are superior to black people. The poorest white person felt better about him or herself because they were treated better than blacks, even when they were called "White Trash." The white establishment, including poor whites in Danville, could not comprehend what it was like to be black.

From the time we were born until the time we died, we were segregated, which does not equate to equality. Black people were born in segregated Winslow Hospital, went to segregated schools and were buried in segregated Oak Hill Cemetery. There were segregated public restrooms, drinking fountains and no form of social respect. Blacks had to sit in the back of the bus and stand at the end of the lunch counter to be served. Everything afforded us was substandard.

Sadly, black people were regarded as 3/5^{ths} human by those who oppressed us. We were chattel—not man or human, but constantly dehumanized. Being treated in this manner meant that we were viewed as objects: soulless, unseen and secondary. We got tired of being called and treated as a "boy" or "gal," which were demeaning terms to us, because we were grown men and women who deserved to have the same respect, rights and freedoms as white people, or any other human beings for that matter.

In 1963, Danville was more agricultural than an industrial community. A large percentage of blacks were sharecroppers

Everything was segregated, including drinking fountains, theaters and waiting rooms.

and worked seasonally in the tobacco factories. Our municipality was segregated from the top to the bottom. There were no blacks employed as clerks, policemen, water meter readers, and not even as truck drivers. When the garbage was collected, the drivers were white, while black men carried the garbage bags to the truck. Dan River Mills was the highest paying employer; however, black people were hired only as janitors. Many blacks were employed as domestic workers, making five dollars a day. I know, because that is what my mother made.

Considering life in Danville for the black community, it is understandable to see how important being an entrepreneur was. In those years of racial segregation, to have one's own business, particularly in a profoundly, racially-oppressive environment, provided a sense of freedom. More critically, those entrepreneurs provided a service out of necessity, as the need was great to serve their long-neglected community, that had encountered racial discrimination from white establishments.

In our community, we had black-owned stores, restaurants, a bank, pharmacy, shoe repair shop, taxi cabs; and we had teachers, doctors, two dentists, morticians, lawyers, contractors, and realtors. Additionally, we had the Ritz Theater. Even though there were five white theaters in downtown Danville, which included the Dan, Lea, Rialto, Virginia and Capitol, blacks could only go to three of those theaters, where they were then relegated to the "colored section," which was another racial slight and example of segregation. The Capitol and Lea theaters did not allow blacks at all.

There were two hotels, the Danville and Leland, which were totally segregated. As a matter of fact, there was not a single hotel from Danville to Richmond, Virginia, where blacks could

Black people were always confronted with segregation and discrimination. It did not matter whether you were a professional or not. If you were black, you were always told to, "Get back!"

stay. Not even Dr. Martin Luther King, Jr. could secure a hotel room in Danville in 1963, as you will read about later.

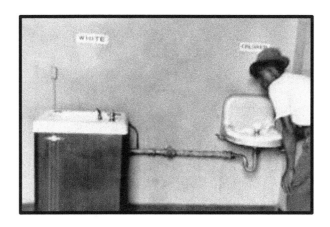

Segregated Water Fountains, 1950
Jim Crow laws were written and enforced by the Democratic Party, 1876-1965.

A typical Klan march in the South against integration. An expression of racial hate.

No More Backseats, Back Doors or Staying Back – A Defining Moment

I was born in Danville, Virginia where I spent my formative years. I attended Grasty Elementary School, Westmoreland Junior High School and Langston High School, until my mother and I moved to Washington, D.C., because she wanted something better for her life and mine.

Like other black people in Danville, I lived on a street behind Main Street, where white folk lived – New Street in North Danville, to be exact. To get across town to Westmoreland and Langston schools and to catch the city bus, you had to walk up to Main Street. Every action in your daily life was always a reminder that white people are in front and blacks are secondary, in essence in the back.

As a black child, you were taught to fear white people, and especially white women—or there would be consequences. If a white woman for whatever reason conjured up a story against a black man and called the police, her side of the story was always believed. We lived in a corrupted, racist judicial system where many innocent black men were imprisoned for free labor to the city and state.

The case of the Martinsville Seven serves as a powerful reminder of the justice system in Virginia, where a group of seven African American men were convicted and executed in 1951 for raping a white woman in 1949 in Martinsville, Virginia (which is 30 miles from Danville). At the time of their arrest, all but one was between the ages of 20 and 23.

It is imperative that we understand racism in that day, because only black men were electrocuted in rape convictions in the state. In fact, before the Martinsville Seven, there were 45 men (all African American) who were executed for rape in

Martinsville Seven

The Virginia Supreme Court of Appeals today agreed to review the cases of seven Martinsville Negroes, sentenced to death for rape.
The seven are, left to right, Booker T. Millner, Frank Hairston, Jr., Howard Lee Hairston, Joe Henry Hampton, John Clabon Taylor, Francis DeSales Grayson and James Luther Hairston.

Virginia since the state began using the electric chair in 1908, where blacks were convicted for attacking white women.

We also feared the police, who protected the white community and were there to keep blacks in "their place". In my youth, I heard testimonies from black men who were brutalized by white police officers for non-violent offenses. Yet, the assault upon our character was not limited to the police.

On station WBTM, there was a radio personality by the name of Leon Smith, who would take articles from the *Danville Register and Bee* about the arrest of blacks. He would use broken English to describe black people as shuffling-along-Negroes, like Amos and Andy, who were Black radio and television personalities of the 40s and 50s. They were depicted as stereotypically slow-talking: "Yassa boss," eyeball-rolling, wide-eyed, ignorant Negroes. The white community saw us as inferior showmen, purposed to entertain them and make them laugh, but they didn't want us to become wise enough to deal with our destiny. It was "racism" personified.

After being honorably discharged from the United States Navy in 1950, I returned to Danville from Washington, D.C., where, in 1953, I came to establish and pastor the Bible Way Church. I was confronted, once again, with the twin demons of segregation and discrimination when my five-year-old daughter, Allethia, and I got on the city bus. During the time that we resided in Washington, D.C., Allethia loved sitting behind the bus driver. However, when she did so in Danville, the response of the driver was blunt and degrading.

"Nigger, get up and go to the back!"

She started to cry, and I did too. On that day, I made up my mind, that if the opportunity ever presented itself, I would do whatever was required of me to change the racist system that I saw and felt that day.

VIRGINIA STATE LAW
REQUIRES ALL
COLORED PASSENGERS
TO RIDE IN REAR OF BUS
CITIZENS RAPID TRANSIT CO.

These are reminders every day that black people were relegated to a place to be behind white folks, so there would be no misunderstanding.

Ten years later, after the incident on the bus, our opportunity came in 1963! Black people constantly encountered institutional racism and a broken judicial system, which still persist today in some ways. However, the barriers were greater then, so undeniably change would have to come! Thus, during the previous year, Reverend L.W. Chase, A.I. Dunlap, Julius Adams and I organized the Danville Christian Progressive Association and became an affiliate of the Southern Christian Leadership Conference.

By 1963, we were prepared to have our defining moment. There would be "no more backseats" when it came to our lives. What occurred next would be monumental for Danville, Virginia, and the nation. Battle lines had been drawn, and the seeds to freedom were planted.

National Protest

As Danville struggles to end segregation and discrimination, there was a national protest going on at the same time. Not only was Danville fed up with the racist system, the spirit of liberation was in the atmosphere.

Martin Luther King, Jr. standing in front of the SCLC office in Atlanta, GA. This headquarters office is where Rev. Dunlap, Rev. Chase and I would talk to Dr. King and Ralph Abernathy about how they could assist us in our efforts in Danville.

Wyatt T. Walker was the executive secretary of the SCLC. He and I became the best of friends. Wyatt was a great professional and an outstanding Freedom Fighter who taught us how to be non-violent. We would meet with Wyatt and his staff to strategize our actions in Danville. *The Author is on the right.*

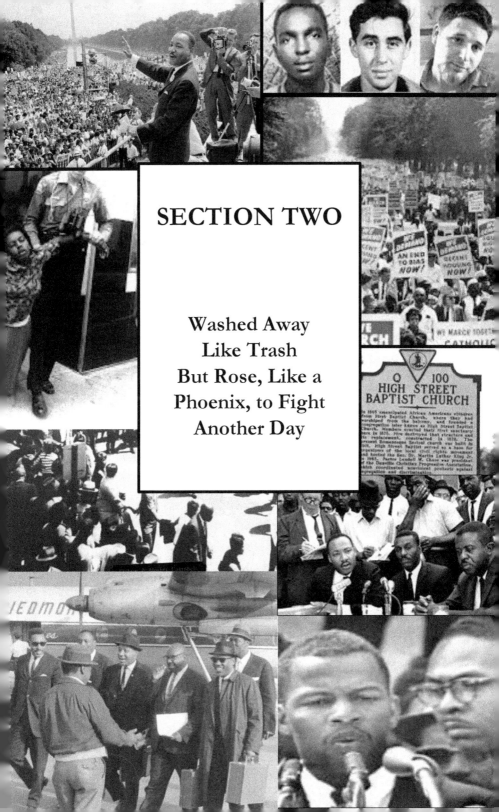

SECTION TWO

Washed Away
Like Trash
But Rose, Like a
Phoenix, to Fight
Another Day

We invited Dr. Martin Luther King, Jr., the most renowned and recognized leader of the Civil Rights Movement, to Danville, and he agreed, giving us that extra boost to shine the light on the treatment of its black community. On March 26th, he spoke directly to the issues of racism. He stated his commitment to support us in our fight for human rights. The City Auditorium was packed with about 2,300 people filling the place, as we were willing and ready to seek justice.

In 1963, I believed in my soul that the hour had come for a change, even if it would have cost my life. The time had come for us to stand up as men, regardless of the consequences. After Dr. King's visit to the city, the black community of Danville was ready for change, and on May 31, 1963, the demonstrations against the two demons, segregation and discrimination, started.

We walked every day, blocked traffic and lied down in the streets, while white people stared, and some made racist remarks. They were demonstrably angry as we walked, carrying placards for rights, justice and equality. Those who came to our marches were not there merely to express their racial hatred, but they also wanted to see if any of their maids, janitors, or Dan River employees were participating. If they were, they were immediately fired.

Women, men, children, old and young demonstrated that day, and no arrests were made until June 5th. The local newspaper ignored us and kept the coverage of the protest from reaching the national press. On June 5, 1963, more than a hundred of us marched into City Hall and went to the City Manager's Office. I was one of the five arrested.

The courtrooms in Danville were segregated, with blacks sitting on one side and whites on the other side. Judge Archibald Aiken, who presided over the Circuit Court, sat with

Martin Luther King, Jr. – Fred Shuttlesworth – Ralph Abernathy

Mass meeting outside Bibleway Church

Demonstrators gather to protest in front of the Municipal Building.

a gun on his side. When I chose to sit where blacks were not supposed to sit, Judge Aiken ordered me to move, and when I did not, he summoned the bailiff, Walter Riddle, to throw me out and down the steps.

I rejoiced for the stand I had taken as I was rolling down the steps! Although Judge Aiken issued a temporary injunction the next day, on June 6, 1963, about 200 people marched to the City Municipal Building, which angered him, because we violated the Court Restraining Order. Therefore, he issued a permanent injunction.

On June 7, 1963, there was a special Grand Jury called by Judge Aiken under the 1859 "John Brown Statue," outlawing "conspiracy to incite the colored population of the State to acts of violence and war against the white population." Considered a felony, our bail was set at $5,500.000 each. A decade would pass before all of us who were indicted were exonerated of the charges from 1963.

On Sunday, June 8, 1963, the Student Non-Violent Coordination Committee (SNCC) sent the field secretaries that I requested to Danville, and the following came: Avon Rollins, SNCC Executive Committee Member, Robert and Dorothy Zellner, and Danny Foss, field secretary. Altogether, there were at least ten SNCC freedom fighters. On June 10th, a day defined as "Bloody Monday," we demonstrated all day, and many were arrested, including Reverend A. I. Dunlap and myself.

There was unrest in the city, because Mayor Julian Stinson and the establishment would not listen to us and blatantly refused to talk with us about our demands, which are outlined in Section Three (Silence Wasn't Golden... Why We Refused to Go Quietly). So on the night of June 10, 1963, 50 demonstrators gathered at Bible Way Church and decided that

Civil Rights marchers attacked with fire hoses on Bloody Monday, June 10, 1963.

Avon Rollins, early 1960s

Avon Rollins, later

Avon Rollins, one of the board members of the Student Nonviolent Coordinating Committee (SNCC) was instrumental in teaching our local protesters how to remain non-violent.

Thurman Echols (front) and **Ernest Smith** (in back) being arrested for violating restraining order.

they would go down to the city jail to pray for those who were incarcerated.

My wife, Gloria, and Reverend H. G. McGhee led the march, and the demonstrators congregated in the corridor between the jail and the Municipal Building. My wife was an eyewitness to everything that occurred that night. The following is her story:

We marched around in the corridor between the jail and the Municipal Building, singing songs such as "Ain't Gonna Let Nobody Turn Me Round" and "We Shall Overcome Some Day." Reverend McGhee had the demonstrators kneel in prayer for those in jail. While they were praying, Chief Eugene McCain said, "Let them have it!" The chief beat me; while many others had concussions. One woman's breast burst open, and the demonstrators were beaten by white, deputized-garbage-collectors, state troopers and the Danville Police. Also, many were attacked by vicious barking dogs. The demonstrators were hosed down to the ground and washed away like trash.

It was an infamous night, during which the blood of innocent citizens was spilled. Many were taken to Winslow Hospital, a medically-inadequate segregated hospital for blacks. An unknown number of people were treated as outpatients by the staff of Winslow Hospital and discharged without a record made detailing their injuries. However, the official record of the Winslow Hospital shows a partial list of some of the demonstrators who were beaten, who are listed below:

June 10, 1963 – Danville, Virginia (Official Record Winslow Hospital

Albert Chambers – Lacerations of head, fractured wrist, possible injury to back

Juanita White – Multiple abrasions on legs and lacerations on knee

Protester arrested on the night of Bloody Monday.

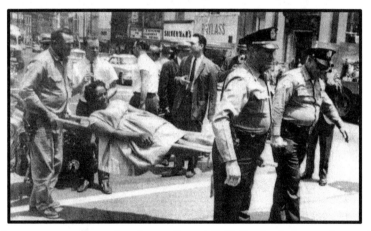

A demonstrator who refused to walk to jail. Police had to carry her to jail.

Gloria Campbell, DCPA Office, 1963

A poster I printed, telling people to boycott the business community.

Barbara Graves – Lacerations of scalp

Richard Coleman – Lacerations of scalp

Hubert Graves – Possible fracture or sprain of left wrist

Mary Graham – Laceration of scalp

Eddie Bethel – Lacerations of scalp

Floyd J. Stone – Possible back injury

Frank Davis – Laceration of scalp

Jessie Warren – Lacerated scalp and possible dislocated shoulder

Charles Russell – Multiple lacerations of scalp

Joe Wilson – Injury to left knee

Ronald Walton – Injury to left shoulder, sacrum and coccyx

Frank Adams – Swollen area right shoulder and complaints of hand hurting

Paul Price – Laceration on right side of head, complaints of dizziness and vomiting

Despite our wounds and injuries, we didn't abandon the struggle. There were enormous attempts to discourage us through violence and legal and political barricades, but we rose up and lived to fight another day.

Until Freedom Rings – The March Goes On!

Danville's white community was very paternalistic and gravely mistaken about the black community, who they viewed as passive. They thought we would not buck the status quo. So when Dr. King and other civil rights icons, including Ralph Abernathy, Wyatt T. Walker, John Lewis, Marion Berry, Fred Shuttlesworth, C.T. Vivian and others came to Danville, the white community called them "outsiders" who were trying to influence us. How wrong they were!

Martin Luther King, Jr. funeral processional in Atlanta, GA, 1968. -My wife and I marched in the Martin Luther King Jr. funeral procession. We are in the second row.

Public Display of Solidarity.
Pastors and leaders marching in Danville.

In actuality, we were challenging the white community in such a way that there was an aberration. The crowning moment of the Civil Rights Movement was in 1963, because it was truly a watershed of motion and all forces coming together to advocate for change. There would be no stopping us until freedom was ours!

In 1960, black students from A&T State University in Greensboro, North Carolina (which is my Alma Mater), sat in protest at the lunch counter in a Woolworth Store (which was off-limits to "colored people"), launching a movement. However, the momentum of the movement was not heightened until 1963, which was a turning point for Civil Rights nationwide.

Attempts made by the local paper could not suppress our story. At the time, the *Danville Register and Bee* newspaper issued two editions of the paper every day. Each edition refused to allow coverage of the marches and the meanness toward black citizens by the white community to reach the Associated Press. Still, we knew the truth would set us free. Nevertheless, it would take years for the City of Danville to admit that the events of June 10, 1963, really occurred and that there were demonstrations going on throughout the year.

In 1963, there was a spirit of freedom in the atmosphere of America that rang out in every city that was segregated, and particularly in the South. The spirit became contagious; it was a spirit of manhood that said that we "were not taking it anymore." It was a great spirit! Black people felt empowered as they had never felt before in my lifetime.

A Sit-In
Demanding to be served in Danville

On the second day of the Greensboro sit-in, **Joseph A. McNeil and Franklin E. McCain are joined by William Smith and Clarence Henderson** at *Woolworth's* lunch counter.

A Year in Review, A Year Like No Other

Little-by-little, our DPCA began testing and pushing racial and judicial barriers in Danville, Virginia, which is documented below. When Dr. King came in March 1963, he was a major impetus to our impending fight; and by May 31st of that year, we began our demonstrations in earnest. The following outlines a continued timeline of events:

In 1962, one year before the mass marching in 1963, we started with the library system in Danville. On Holbrook Street, there was the William F. Grasty Library, "For blacks only," and on the corner of Main Street and Holbrook Avenue, while there was the Confederate Library, "For whites only."

Reverend Doyle Thomas, Reverend A. I. Dunlap, Julius Adams and I chose to go to the all-white library, and the end result of our protest was that the City of Danville gave us vertical integration—in that all of the chairs and tables were removed, and everyone had to stand and read.

On January 1, 1963, Reverend Dunlap and I went to the Howard Johnson Restaurant, located on Route 29 South. When Dunlap and I went into the restaurant, we sat down, and we were refused service. A white employee came to our booth and began pushing a mop with a scrub bucket with ammonia, which was burning our eyes. Thereafter, we were arrested and fined $100 each.

When Dr. King came to Danville for the first time in March of 1963, we went to the Holiday Inn on Riverside Drive after he had spoken. The hotel denied him a room because of the color of his skin. Undeterred, we left Danville and drove Dr. King to Greensboro, North Carolina, and he was given a room at the Holiday Inn at Circle Mall. That night for me was unforgettable!

Danville, Ballou Park, was for "white only."
However, if you were a maid with your uniform on
to nurse a white child, you were accepted.

When we protested and violated restraining orders,
we would go limp, as a refusal to accept the status
quo. We were carried to jail as a protest.

As we sat with Dr. King that night until about 3:00 a.m., he became very relaxed and removed his shirt and put on his pajama top. We could see the scar where he had been stabbed by a demented woman in New York at a book signing.

"Campbell," he said, "you see this scar where I was stabbed? If I had sneezed, I would have lost my life."

Tragically, five years later, Dr. King *would* lose his life to an assassin's bullet on April 4, 1968, in Memphis, Tennessee, where he was marching, standing and protesting with sanitation workers. Despite living only 39 years, he left a powerful legacy of humanity in the fight for racial and social justice. He was a brilliant presence that elevated us to continue the fight, because we would need it in our long, arduous journey for equality.

A few years before Dr. King's death, he led what would be called "Bloody Sunday" in Selma, Alabama, which occurred in March 1965. Before that, there was Danville's version of a bloodbath and mass beatings of demonstrators, called "Bloody Monday," which occurred on June 10, 1963. It was a critical event in 1963 Civil Rights history.

On June 11, 1963, Danville's City Council enacted an ordinance to limit the time, place, and size of picketing and demonstrations. However, on that same day, Reverend L.W. Chase, pastor of High Street Baptist Church and President of the Danville Christian Progressive Association, led a group of 200 demonstrators to City Hall to protest the police brutality from the night before, and to again assert the need for equal employment. Many of those who walked slowly up and down the sidewalk in front of City Hall wore bandages on their heads and arms, and one young man walked with a crutch. However, Mayor Stinson refused to meet with us.

High Street Baptist Church was the headquarters of our civil rights movement. I recall one night, we were in the church, the doors were locked, and Danville Police kicked the doors down, came in and arrested us. They had no respect for the "house of worship."

High Street Baptist Church circa 1884

In 1865, emancipated African Americans withdrew from First Baptist Church, where they had worshiped in the balcony, and founded a congregation later known as High Street Baptist Church. Members erected their first building here in 1873. Fire destroyed that structure and its replacement, constructed in 1878. The present Romanesque Revival church was built in 1901. High Street Baptist served as a base for organizers of the local civil rights movement and hosted the Rev. Martin Luther King Jr. in 1963. Pastor Lendell W. Chase was president of the Danville Christian Progressive Association, which coordinated nonviolent protests against segregation and discrimination.

Three days later, on June 13th, Reverend Chase again led about 250 marchers to City Hall to speak to the Mayor. The crowd waited on the steps, as Reverend Chase, Reverend Dunlap, Julius Adams and I tried to get into City Hall. Due to the fact that the doors were locked, we decided to stay on the steps, and everyone agreed to stay all night, if necessary, to see the mayor. Women from High Street Baptist Church and other ladies from the community brought food for the demonstrators. Despite our efforts, the mayor still refused to talk to us.

I shall never forget the humiliation from the Danville Police Department when they went to Rev Chase's home to arrest him for violating the restraining order. The police officers knocked on the door and Mrs. Chase told them that Rev Chase was taking a shower. They took him out of the shower and Rev Chase put on his wife's housecoat and was taken to jail. After the arraignment, he walked from the court back to his home barefoot, with nothing on but the housecoat.

On June 17, 1963, with the support of SNCC, we went to New York and staged a protest, with over 100 people marching. We urged the promotion of black Americans and the use of corporate power to force Danville to accede to our demands. One of the largest employers in our city was Dan River Mills, a company which refused to hire blacks in positions no higher than what was considered minimal and menial.

A few months after our protest in New York, *The New York Times*, in an article dated on August 11, 1963, cited Danville's defense tactics, stating:

"White authorities in Danville, Virginia, defense strategy (against Civil Rights protesters), is among the most unyielding, ingenious legalistic, and effective of any city in the South."

Martin Luther King Jr. arrives for one of his four visits to Danville in 1963. Clockwise, from center: Martin Luther King, Jr., Rev L.W. Chase, A.I. Dunlap (partially-hidden), Bernard Lee (Dr. King's assistant), Percy Walters (facing group), Lawrence Campbell and HG McGhee.

This is a publication of the Student Non-violent Coordinating Committee that helped to get our struggle in the national media.

When the Grand Jury held its hearings the week prior to June 21st, no person subpoenaed was allowed to bring a lawyer. Attorney Len Holt of Norfolk, Virginia, had handled most of the cases. He, too, spent three days in jail after he was served with the indictment in the courtroom. Len Holt and other lawyers asked that all pending cases be placed in the jurisdiction of the Federal Court. They complained that Judge A. M. Aiken, who had tried cases, walked into the courtroom wearing a gun, which clearly was intimidating and dangerous.

On June 21, 1963, the Grand Jury indicted more of the Civil Rights leaders under the 1859 statue, which included officials of SCLC's Virginia Chapter, and Students of the Non-Violent Coordinating Committee, including Milton Reid, the state's representative for SCLC.

On July 11, 1963, Dr. King came back to Danville and spoke to a large gathering at the High Street Baptist Church. What a message he gave that night! He spoke boldly about police brutality in Danville.

On August 25, 1963, ten "colored" students entered the Danville Public Schools System under the order of the State Pupil Placement Board which was a positive beginning in education. Those students were:

Edger Drew Adams
Julius Emmanuel Adams, Jr.
Yvonne Teressa Adams
Elaine Elizabeth Chase
Allethia Yvonne Campbell
Angela Joyce Campbell
Glendora Chase
Larry Wendell Chase
Cynthia Anita Muse
George Edward Pinchback

The March on Washington

John Lewis speech during March on Washington on August 28, 1963. "If Congress doesn't pass meaningful Civil Rights legislation…

U.S. Rep. John Lewis (D-GA) receiving the 2010 Medal of Freedom by President Barack Obama "If somebody told me one day I would be standing in the White House, and an African American president presenting me the Medal of Freedom, I would have said, 'Are you crazy'? Are you out of your mind?"

John Lewis was a strong supporter of our efforts in Danville. He came to us at a time when we needed his encouragement.

My daughter, Allethia, entered George Washington High School, and my middle child, Angela, went to G.L.H. Johnson Elementary School, where she was the only black child in the school at that time. This was a major shift in the educational system of our city.

On August 28,1963, buses and cars left Danville to go to the March on Washington, D.C. John Lewis said in his speech,

"If Congress does not pass meaningful civil rights legislation, SNCC will march through the streets of Jackson, Danville, Cambridge, and Birmingham…"

On October 6, 1963, we pushed the business community to desegregate hotels, restaurants, theaters, and the hiring of blacks as clerks. In addition, we pushed the City of Danville to integrate Ballou Park and to appoint Blacks to city boards, as well as to the police and fire departments. It was October 16, 1963, that Chief McCain announced the hiring of William T. Terry, the first black policeman since Reconstruction. This was a fulfillment of one of our demands to the city, which was another turning point in Danville, with more to come.

By the time Dr. King came back to Danville on November 16, 1963, we had made many efforts to upend the status quo. During Dr. King's visit, I remember him at High Street Baptist Church; where he shared the pulpit with an avowed Nazi, who tried to interrupt his speech. Patient, Dr. King let him have his say. Five days later, Dr. King came back to Danville, on November 21, 1963, and he told the City of Danville that we meant business.

A day later, the world mourned the assassination of President John F. Kennedy, on November 22, 1963. The black community loved President John F. Kennedy, and his death, in a strange way, gave the freedom fighters greater determination to defeat racism.

March on Washington

President J.F. Kennedy meeting with leaders of the March on Washington at the White House on Aug 28, 1963. From second left are Whitney Young, National Urban League, Dr. Martin Luther King, Jr., Christian Leadership Conference, John Lewis, SNCC, Rabbi Joachim Prinz, American Jewish Congress, Dr. Eugene Donnaly, National Council of Churches, A. Philip Randolph, AFL-CIO, Kennedy, Walter Reuther, UAW, Lyndon B. Johnson and Roy Wilkins, NAACP.

"The ultimate tragedy is not the oppression and cruelty by the bad people, but the silence over that by the good people."

Dr. Martin Luther King, Jr.

Freedom Fighters, Guardians and Angels

To attain the level of freedom we have today, many people were beaten, went to jail and literally laid out in the streets, with blood seeping from wounds sustained while under attack from the batons and fire hoses of those who vehemently opposed civil rights for the black community. All of what we endured was for this generation and for generations to come to be free. The support and involvement of Dr. Martin Luther King, Jr. and some members of the SCLC, SNCC, who came to Danville, were extremely instrumental to the Civil Rights Movement, not only in our city, but throughout the country.

We were grateful for every voice, prayer and person who risked their lives for freedom. Those on the national and local levels of the Civil Rights Movement made a stand and did what they could to combat the unyielding oppression of black lives from proponents of suppression and segregation. They were our freedom fighters, guardians and angels.

There were also some people who lived in the Danville community who gave so much to defeat segregation. Some of them were: Reverend L. W. Chase of High Street Baptist Church, Reverend A. I. Dunlap of Saint Paul AME Church, Reverend Doyle Thomas of Loyal Baptist Church, Reverend H.G. McGhee of Greater Triumph Missionary Baptist Church, Julius Adams (he filed a successful discrimination suit against Dan River Mills), Ernest Smith, a cab driver, Prophet Cobbs, Mrs. Beatrice Hairston, a school teacher who lodged Dr. King and Ralph Abernathy in her house, Arthur Pinchback, Jr. and Sr., Duke Bennett who put up bonds for demonstrators, William Pritchett, Irvin Burton and Reverend Thurman Echols.

We also must remember the black and white lawyers who played a most important role in defending us nationally in the various levels of our judicial system, such as: Ruth Harvey, A.C.

A protester carrying a placard for whites and blacks to come together. It is a simple expression with a powerful meaning.

Sit-ins in variety stores did not stop, but we continued to demand equality.

Muse, Charity, Harry Woods, Jerry L. Williams, Sr., Samuel Tucker from Richmond, Bill Kunstler, Arthur Kenoy from New York, and Len Holt of Norfolk, who put our struggle before their own law practice.

During the heat of our struggle, I met Charles Womack, whom I will never forget for his boldness and the inner strength that he exhibited in fighting for human justice in spite of the ostracism and criticism that he and his family endured.

As a prominent white businessman in the community, he was highly respected. When he saw the blatant bias that *The Register and Bee* demonstrated in reporting a one-sided picture of events, condemning the black community and its leaders during the Danville Civil Rights demonstrations. Charles bought the *Commercial Appeal* newspaper so that, in its publication, the truth could be told. Nevertheless, June 10th, also known as "Bloody Monday," was a pivotal moment in Danville towards integration, and it took Danville more than three decades to finally admit that this infamous night of violence happened.

For his integrity, Charles Womack was called a "nigger-lover," "a turn-coat" and other egregious names in an attempt to demean him. However, he was a man of great character who was strong and steadfast in his determination to reveal what city officials would not admit – that the brutal beating of the Civil Rights demonstrators was true, and that they suffered mightily at the hands of those in the white community, who defiantly tried to block their path to freedom.

Charles and I remained friends until his death. We could not have achieved any semblance of success without people like him and others in the white community, like Mrs. Virginia Bourne, Dr. Samuel Newman and Mother Teresa of the local Catholic Church, who stood boldly with us.

Charles Womack

For his integrity, Charles Womack was called a **"nigger-lover,"** a "turn-coat," and other egregious names in an attempt to demean him. However, he was a man of great character who was strong and steadfast in his determination to reveal what city officials would not admit.

Dr. Samuel Newman was an outspoken Jewish community member for civil rights. He was brave and courageous and caused many so-called friends to brand him as a nigger-lover. He stood with us and was not afraid! He was one in the white community that God sent to us in the height of our struggle to gain our civil rights.

Dr. Samuel Newman

Mother Teresa

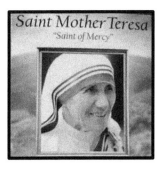

Saint Mother Teresa
"Saint of Mercy"

Mother Teresa was a nun in the local Catholic Church. She attended our mass meetings and marched with us in protest. Even though her Catholic Leaders rebuked her, it did not deter nor stop her from speaking out against the racist white people in the community.

Those on the national and local levels of the Civil Rights movement made a stand and did what they could to combat the unyielding oppression of black lives from proponents of suppression and segregation. They were our freedom fighters, guardians and angels.

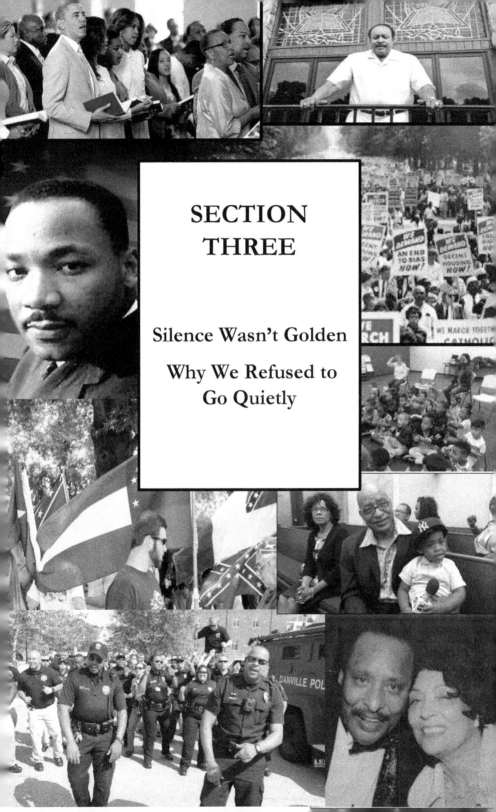

SECTION THREE

Silence Wasn't Golden

Why We Refused to Go Quietly

We weren't living. Rather, we were existing in a system that treated us as inferior. There could be no more silence. Our voices rose together as one to demand what was due us. Yet our demands were only the beginning. Reaching five levels of power would also be an integral factor in bringing the black community to the table of opportunity and prosperity.

The Civil Rights Movement in our city did not simply occur, without planning and thoughtfulness. In 1963, we appealed to Mayor Julian Stinson and the city manager before we demonstrated. They would not listen nor grant us any of our demands, which we clearly outlined. We wanted:

1. Blacks employed in the municipality on an equal basis, and not denied jobs solely because of race;

2. Appointments of blacks to boards and commissions;

3. The hiring of black policemen and firemen;

4. The implementation of the decision by the Supreme Court in Brown verses the Board of Education, to integrate schools NOW!

5. The integration of seating arrangements in the courts of the city;

6. The integration of Ballou Park;

7. The integration of cemeteries;

8. The elimination of segregated seating arrangements on the buses of Danville Transit Company;

9. The integration of Danville Memorial Hospital.

Attorney Len Holt filed an omnibus suit that sued the city for the eradicating of segregation within the municipality.

The Powers that Be

There were five areas in our struggle that we hoped to bring about change and they were:

Danville Memorial Hospital

The hospital was segregated, and black people could only go there as a janitor or a maid, but never admitted as a patient.

Paula Martin Smith tells a first-person account of helping to integrate the Danville bus system. At age 10, Smith was asked to move to another seat after taking one behind the driver. "I'm comfortable where I am," she repeatedly told the driver, who went on to call the police. It was a move that led her father, Maceo Martin, to sue the city. He was at the time the President of First State Bank.

Matt Bell/*Register and Bee*

1. The Power of the Vote

The Voting Rights Act was signed into law by President Lyndon Baines Johnson on August 6, 1965, aimed to overcome the illegal barriers at state and local levels that prevented black Americans from exercising their right to vote under the 15th Amendment (1870) to the Constitution of the United States. This was another turning point in the political body of Danville and the nation.

In Virginia, if you were black, you had to pay a $1.50 poll tax to vote, while in other states black voters had to recite the Constitution of the United States or know how many beans were in a jar in order to exercise the right to vote.

Anything and everything was done to stop blacks from voting. Were it not for the Voting Rights Act, we would not have had the first black President of United States, Barack Obama, or the first black Governor of the State of Virginia, Douglas Wilder.

In 1963, we began to fight for our basic rights, where voting and representation were critical elements. Moreover, on the national level, we would not have had the first black Attorney General of the United States, Eric Holder and the second black Attorney General, Loretta Lynch, from Durham, North Carolina, and the two women who President Obama nominated to the Supreme Court, Sonia Sotomayor and Elena Kagan.

Currently, we have four blacks on the School Board, and the Superintendent is black. My youngest son, Philip, was one of the members. There are three blacks on City Council. My oldest son, Larry, is one of the three, and the Mayor is black. We also have the first black City Treasurer. The Deputy City Manager is black, and there are many other important positions that here-to-fore were not given to blacks.

Barack Obama
The first black President
of the United States.

Douglas Wilder
The first black Governor of
the State of Virginia

Phillip Campbell
Former School
Board Member

Alonzo Jones
Mayor

Lawrence Campbell, Jr.
City Councilman

Jeffrey Hubbard
School Board Member

Sheila Branch
First African American
Treasurer in Danville

Without having the power to vote, we would not have had in our city, the first black mayor, Charles Harris. Nor would we have had the first black School Board member, Harry Waller and I, the first black Chairman of the Danville School Board.

Now that we have the vote, it is critical to maintain and exercise our rights. An example of letting down our guard came as a result of the election of President Barack Obama. Many of us saw it as a "kumbaya moment," that is, we thought that everything was going to be all right for black people. As a result, we relaxed and acted like we were in the Promised Land, but that was not the case.

When Barack Obama won the presidency, conservatives were incensed that a black man had ascended to the highest position in the United States and that he was able to accomplish what former Presidents tried and failed in giving to America Universal Health Care.

For anyone who thinks that racism is dead, they only have to observe what is happening in many southern states. In North Carolina, gerrymandering is an issue, and political unrest is stoking the flames of racism across a divided nation, which is why we must continue to VOTE, protest, protect our rights and strive to do and be better.

Medgar Evers, James Chaney, Andrew Goodman, Michael Schwerner, and other unsung heroes and heroines were denied or killed for their advocacy for this most basic and powerful right for black people. This cannot be taken for granted for fear of reverting completely back to yesteryear and the steady denigration of the gains we made before, in and after 1963 in positioning ourselves to use the ballot box to make inroads to political power.

Voting in Virginia after the repeal of the
Poll Tax circa 1966.

Ivanhoe Donaldson, Board Member, Student Non-Violent
Coordinating Committee (SNCC), **Marion Barry,** civil activist,
and James Forman, President of Congress of Racial Equality
(CORE) in Danville, Virginia, June 1963, Danny Lyon, *Memories
of the Southern Civil Rights Movement.*

2. The Power of Economics

There are more than 330 million people in America and of that demographic, there are more than 56 million Hispanics or 17% of the American population. There are more than 37 million black people in America or 12% of the American population. There are 21 black-owned banks in America today, with assets totaling approximately 4.7 billion dollars, or approximately .43 percent of African America's 1.2 trillion dollars in buying power. In 1994, there were 54 black-owned banks in America, according to the FDIC. Now there are only 21.

Many of those banking institutions are defunct, such as Freedom Bank in New York City, Consolidated Bank in Richmond, Virginia, Atlantic Bank in Norfolk, Virginia, and Imperial Savings and Loan in Martinsville, Virginia. In summary, we have lost 34 black-owned banks in 23 years. That's more than one bank per year. Most recently, the first and only black-owned bank, First State Bank of Danville, has become Movement Bank.

Black businesses start-ups that are now closed suffered that fate largely because they did not get the support from their community. For example, why is the black community supporting white funeral establishments, when white people do not send their deceased family members to black mortuaries?

The black community must support black-owned banks and businesses. I am talking about buying shares and investing in the banks. The question is, why doesn't the black community support black businesses? Sadly, we criticize and find fault and reasons not to do business with black-owned companies, who still need the support of their community.

Cashiers conduct business with customers at **First State Bank on Union Street in Danville**.
Contributed photo from History United

Virginia Center for Digital History - University of Virginia
Intersecting Networks: **First State Bank Board Members**.

The Hispanic community, which is now the second largest community of people in the United States, support each other and have their own banks, clothing stores, salons, restaurants and voting power. They are working together and are a force to reckon with. Even the U.S government understands economic power when they see it.

When black people were selling bootleg liquor to survive in the days of economic depression and were caught, they were given hard time in prison. The government saw how much money it could make selling liquor, so they legalized selling liquor and started the A.B.C stores.

In order to survive, black people would write numbers even though it was illegal. When the government saw how much money was made in number writing, they legalized gambling by calling it the lottery.

Many of our black brothers are in prison because they were given excessive sentences for using or trafficking marijuana. When the government saw how much money could be made in selling marijuana, they legalized it and said that it can be sold for recreational or medical use. Those blacks who are serving time for the use of marijuana should to be released from prison now!

Today, states like Colorado can't keep enough marijuana in stock because of the great demand. I say, let all of those black brothers and sisters who are in prison for using or selling marijuana out of jail today, right now, and provide viable opportunities to cultivate their minds and contribute to the betterment of society.

3. The Power of The Black Family

In 1712, the slave masters brought a white man to America from the West Indies by the name of Willie Lynch, for the sole

The incarceration rates of black men far exceeded that of white men. Many of our brothers were given extensive penalties that could not be justified in a fair legal system.

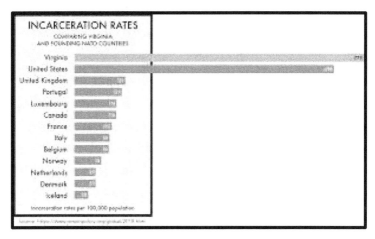

A typical sight of a black man behind bars.

Many of our black brothers were unfairly found guilty because the state would use black men to work for the state without monetary compensation for their labor.

purpose of teaching the slave masters how to control the black slaves. Slaves were running away, and many were killed. Willie Lynch taught the slave masters psychological control over the slaves.

"Turn the young blacks against the old blacks," he said, "and the old blacks against the young blacks. Pit the 'house light-skinned' blacks against the 'brown-skinned' blacks in the yard and turn the brown-skinned blacks against the 'black-skinned' blacks in the field."

He conveyed that it was important that blacks distrusted each other and became jealous and envious of each other. "Teach them to depend on the white slave master," he added and assured that if this strategy worked for a year, it would work for a lifetime.

Apparently, it is still working, as documented by Lori Tharps, who is a professor of journalism at Temple University. She wrote about the issues of racism and colorism in society, which is not just in the black community but is prevalent around the world.

According to Tharps, "skin color will continue to serve as the most obvious criterion in determining how a person will be evaluated and judged. In this country, because of deeply-entrenched racism, we already know that dark skin is demonized, and light skin wins the prize. And that occurs precisely because this country was built on principles of racism. It cannot be overstated that if racism didn't exist, a discussion about varying skin hues would simply be a conversation about aesthetics."

Tharps goes on to refer to a quote by Alice Walker, the great author of African American descent who is best known for her Pulitzer Prize winning book, *The Color Purple*. Walker defined colorism as "prejudicial or preferential treatment of same-race people, based solely on their color." Light-skin preference had

People in High Street Baptist Church listening to SNCC discussion after being beaten, 1963, Danny Lyons.

The murders of Chaney, Goodman, and Schwerner, also known as the Freedom Summer murders, the Mississippi Civil Rights Workers' murders or the Mississippi Burning murders, involved three activists who were abducted and murdered in Neshoba County, Mississippi in June 1964 during the Civil Rights Movement.

been common practice in the black community for generations, but Walker gave it a name and marked it as an evil that must be stopped in order for African Americans to progress as a people.

During slavery, black mothers and fathers were separated from their children, and families disbanded in record numbers. Many of our black families were more matriarchal (led by single mothers) than patriarchal.

We have too many teenage pregnancies, fathers deserting their families and the lack of parental involvement in education. Black men comprise 6% of the American population, but 50% of the prison population is black. Unemployment is up 9 to 16% for blacks and even higher for black teenagers. For black women in prison, many of them are mothers, having babies born in prison with psychological wounds.

The overall quality of black life is in peril, when heart disease among blacks is 4% higher than the average American. For housing, 1.3% of African Americans have lost their homes; and 40% of all blacks live in poverty. In our families, many of our black men are on the down-low, involved in sex with men. Forty-six percent of them are infected with AIDS, and AIDS is the leading cause of death for black women between the ages of 25 -34.

So the question is not only if "Black Lives Matter." It also entails "whether the condition of black families matter," and if black families can survive the myriad challenges that play an integral role in its potential demise?

More pointedly, if Black Lives Matter, why would men transmit the deadly virus of AIDS to our sisters? Does black life really matter when in many of our families there is widespread, domestic violence? There are too many black men

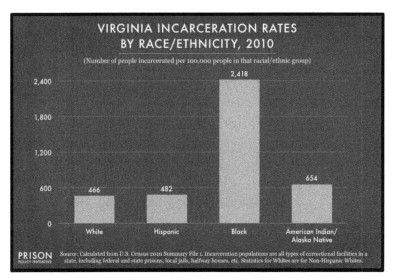

This statistic from 2010 shows there is much more to be done in our judicial system.

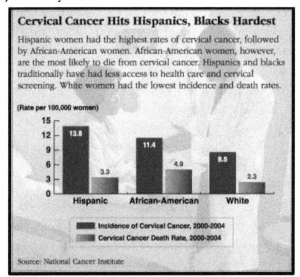

Many of our black women are in prison and having babies during their incarceration. Some of the children have psychological challenges.

who are inflicting rage against our women. If black life matters, then why are we molesting our little black girls and boys?

Does black life only matter when a white policeman kills a black person? We become alarmed when a white policeman kills a black person, but it's amazing that our killing of each other has been going on for years and there seems to be no major outcry. Why is that?

The destruction of the black family is accelerated by the killing of blacks by blacks, which is still happening in cities across the United States, but none more notable than Chicago. The deaths are so common that the media has almost stopped reporting them in the national media. Do you think that would happen in the white community?

In 2016, there were 713 murders committed in Chicago. Seventy-one percent (71%) of the murderers were black; and of those murdered, 75% were black. That is about 9 black lives, "precious and unique," killed per week, which equates to a devastating loss of human potential, senelessly wasted.

So far this year, three blacks have been killed and 27 blacks have been shot and wounded in Chicago, which is a number that is sure to increase, if we continue killing each other. It has become an epidemic that has to stop in the name of all humanity and for the sake of self-preservation of the black community!

I believe if Dr. King were alive today and saw what we are doing to each other, he would have a nightmare instead of the "Dream" that he envisioned more than 50 years ago. When our fore parents were enslaved, the slave master killed our people. After we were freed from slavery, the Ku Klux Klan killed many of our people and others who fought for human rights. But today, the slave master is not killing us and the Ku Klux Klan is not killing us. We are killing each other. So I ask, "Does black life matter?" Yes, it does. For that matter, all life matters

Ku Klux Klan Cross Burning

The KKK is not our worst enemy. WE are our own worst enemy! The question that needs to be answered is "Why are we destroying each other, wasting potential leaders?

Danville, VA: Triangle IWW joins with other Antifa groups to **Shut Down the KKK**. The Triangle-Industrial Workers of the world came to Danville to help fight against White Supremacy.

but we must preserve and honor our strong legacy of endurance in the face of adversity.

4. The Power of Education

The right that the black community has attained to access an education has been critical. In addition, it has been a cornerstone to many advances to our participation in politics, medicine, business and other facets of life. However, we paid a steep price for this privilege, including countless marches, protests, human suffering, public humiliation, beatings, and even deaths.

Many of our people are taking advantage of educational opportunities, and some are not. The Emancipation Proclamation set the slaves physically free, but education is the only means by which we can become psychologically free.

At the last banquet in which Dr. King spoke, he said, "The black man has been freed from the chains and shackles of slavery, but not free from the chains of the mind." Access to education was and still is a major turning point in defeating racism. It's been more than 60 years since the Supreme Court ruled in Brown vs. the Board of Education that "separate but equal" education was unconstitutional. That decision was a watershed moment in education, turning the country toward the integration of public education.

Even though the decision to integrate the schools was the law of the land in 1954, it took Danville nine years before it would integrate its schools, in 1963. Sometimes, I think that we forget that when we fought for Civil Rights, which included access to public accommodations, voting rights, etc., those rights were already in the Constitution, but we were denied those rights solely based on race. The laws were not changed; we just demanded that we be given our Civil Rights. However,

Thurgood Marshall, Brown vs. Board of Education, 1954

Our Black Educators

One of the most important groups of people in our struggle for equality, diversity and inclusion, in 1963, were our black teachers. They insisted with a parental approach, that all of us would get the best education possible. They did not have many of the tools that the white teachers had to enhance us. However, in spite of that, they somehow created means to help us to become productive citizens. For me, and I believe I speak for others, I'm sure our black teachers cared about us. History has shown us what they did to develop our minds.

All of us should look at leaders, past and present, that sat at the feet of these great educators. They were underpaid, but they stood the test of time. Thank God for our black educators!

Lawrence G. Campbell, Sr.

in the black community, we still have young people dropping out of school, which is a disgrace in the face of those who made sacrifices to integrate schools. It is painful that graduation among blacks is not increasing. We continue to fight the battle of drop-outs, in-school suspensions and expulsions.

We admire our former president, Barack Obama. However, his becoming president did not just happen. He prepared himself at Harvard School of Law, and his wife went to Princeton University. Both are lawyers. They were ready for the moment. Education does that. It prepares individuals for the moment when the opportunity presents itself so that they are ready for the challenge. We must remember that the quality of our preparation determines the quality of our performance.

We fought for school integration and sacrificed much. Today, when I see black children drop out of school, they are doing what the slave-masters wanted us to do. Ignorance will keep you as a mental slave, living on an asphalt plantation. That is why slave masters were unapologetic about keeping their chattel from reading and learning, because they knew that an educated mind was one that was empowered and severely threatened their ability to "control" and exercise their "will" over their slaves.

Once the oppressed realized that they were as smart and deserving or more so than their oppressors, it transformed the playing field for racial justice and equality. Education is powerful because it helps one understand the social and political systems of the times. The hiring of the first black School Superintendent in Danville and having witnessed the second black School Superintendent succeeding was phenomenal.

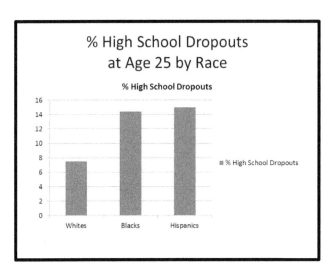

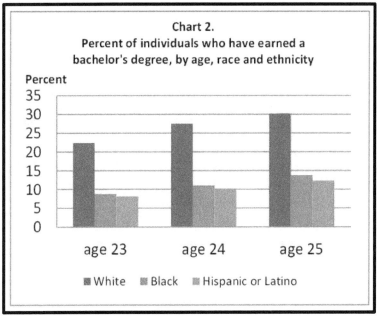

5. The Power of the Black Church

The Black Church is the cornerstone of political activity in the black community and has been so throughout history. Take the Black Church out of the social equation and what do you have? The Black Church has always led the fight for Civil Rights of black people. Had it not been for the Black Church and the black preacher, the social revolution would not have been successful. Dr. Martin Luther King, Jr, C.T. Vivian, John Lewis, Ralph Abernathy, Jesse Jackson, and Fred Shuttlesworth are all black preachers.

In 1963, just as it was in times of slavery, the black preacher spoke truth to power and preached a gospel of liberation. While the White Church was silent on the issue of integration. Reverend R. J. Barber, Jr., Attorney John Carter and others vehemently opposed us. They called Dr. Martin Luther King, Jr. a "communist" and a "rabble rouser."

The White Church and white people in our community are going to stick together. The white man and white community do not want to sit under the leadership of a black leader, be he a black preacher or the President of the United States.

It does not matter if you are high-yellow, educated, a lawyer, a doctor or a preacher—you are still black. You can run to the White Church, but you are still black.

President Obama knows this to be true, because he experienced racial challenges as president, as well as before he attained the highest office in the land. He said that when he went to the store before he became the President, he would be watched by the clerk, as if he was about to steal something. He said that he could hear car doors lock as he passed by white passengers.

It is amazing that blacks still sit under the ministry of a white pastor, but they will come to the black preacher for assistance

Local civil rights leader Bishop Lawrence Campbell said he will never forget the times Martin Luther King Jr. came to Danville.

Reverend   Jerimiah   Wright and   **U.S. Presidential candidate Barack Obama, 2008**.

in racial matters. When black preachers tell those black persons to go to their white pastors, their remarks have always been, "he does not understand."

One Sunday morning in 1963, Reverend Thurman Echols, Deacon Cole Cain, some others and I went to the Baptist Tabernacle Church when it was on East Thomas Street. R. J. Barber, Jr. was the pastor, and when we sat on the pew, the white congregants moved off the pew. When we left the church, there were deacons at the door who said, "Niggers, don't come back here anymore!"

The White Church preached a gospel of separation of races, which it commonly did during the era of slavery. The white preacher made the slave master feel justified in his mistreatment and killing of slaves. This made the white slave owner feel that he was going to heaven, because the slaves were seen as chattel and not "human beings" held in bondage.

In general, the White Church failed to condemn slavery, and even used passages in the Bible to justify and maintain the evil institution. The white pulpit was silent then and is silent now when it comes to Racial Profiling, the Black Life Matters Movement, White Supremacy, the Confederate Flag, the K.K.K. and any of the struggles black people face. The white pulpit made the Ku Klux Klan feel no guilt for the lynching of black people.

When the white community speaks of people of color, they are talking as though white is not a color. It's because they see white as supreme – not as a color. They do not see themselves a color. On national news, they address people of color meaning "black" or "brown."

The hypocrisy of the white preacher in the days of segregation and discrimination was clearly magnified when he sent white missionaries to Africa to evangelize the so-called "Black heathen." Afterward, they would applaud themselves

White Evangelicals have remained solidly behind Donald J. Trump, despite his numerous racist statements about black people, sexual assault accusations and outright lies to the American People.

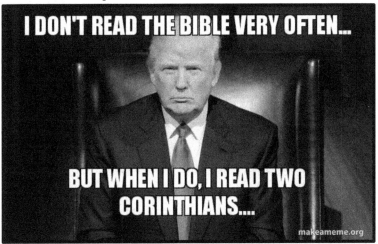

Donald Trump uses the Bible and conservative whites and some blacks to his own political advantage. He has shown us that he is a racist and speaks in coded language that the hate groups of America enjoy and understand… people like David Duke, the head of the KKK.

and give praise about how many Africans accepted Jesus Christ. Those same missionaries would then return to America and support the separation of the races in church and public accommodations. They did not see racism as a sin. The same Africans that they say were saved could not sit beside them and worship in unity in their American church congregation.

The power of the Black Church in regard to politics has not dissipated, as white politicians who want to try to secure the black vote still often seek out black congregations. So the Black Church is still a force and the voice for social justice. The Black Church also has been an advocate for education in our communities. There are 117 Historically Black colleges and universities today, and 37% were started in the basement of black churches. In 1963, the so called "Christian Schools" were established and grew as a way of combating school integration. Preachers, such as the late Jerry Falwell, built Liberty University in Lynchburg, Virginia, on the back of racism. Blacks could not attend Liberty's Christian School. It was the same in Danville, as Reverend R. J. Barber, Jr. played a major role in fighting to maintain segregated schools and was adamantly opposed to Dr. Martin Luther King, Jr. and the Civil Rights Movement.

A Dream Deferred – A Nation Divided?

It is imperative to understand that all that we wanted in 1963 was equal treatment under the law in our struggle for Civil Rights, which is still necessary to fight for now, lest we lose all of the gains we worked so hard to secure more than five decades ago. One of the greatest achievements was due to demanding and then asserting our right to vote and be educated.

Former President Obama shares reflections on the Power of the Black Church – West Angeles Church.

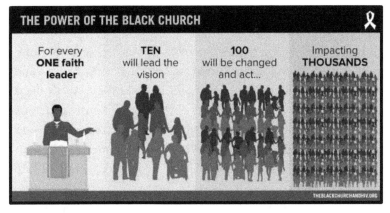

The black church is the liberation voice of the black community. What is amazing to me is how black folks join white congregations, and white people do not join black churches. Why is that? When you see white people in our congregation, they are there because they are dating or married to a black person, or they are a politician looking for a vote.

The fight for equality has humanized us to many who had no exposure to African Americans or who had no understanding about our plight to be viewed as equals. In time, these factors caused a cataclysmic shift in the most desired result, which was putting a black person in the White House.

Many never thought they would live to see the day when someone of African ancestry would be the most powerful leader of the free world, emerging as the president of the United States.

Even today, we are dealing with the hydra of racism that still has its tentacles in everything that we do. Sometimes overt, but in many instances very covert. Racism has taken on a different facade now. In 1963, the racist would let you know who they were and where they stood. Not so today. Racists could be wearing three-piece suits and will shake a black man's hand, go to lunch with him and sit on boards with him. That is as far as it goes, because it is all job-related, with no effort to develop a friendship.

Since 1963, the judicial system has gotten worse in that one in four black men will end up in prison. That remains an issue to be addressed and obliterated. In other areas of deep concern, the Confederate Flag continues to fly in the face of the black community, and there are those who are still fighting the Civil War. We still have a segment of white people who embrace the KKK, Alt-Right, Neo-Nazis and White Supremacists.

We must also remember that when Barack Obama was elected President; it did not take long for the racists to hold meetings to try to stop him. The conservatives called Universal Health Care "Obamacare." We should not call it Obamacare, because this terminology makes a mockery of what the President has done. Besides many other victories and accomplishments of President Obama that have already been

On March 23, 2010, President Barack Obama signed federal statue **The Affordable Care Act** (also known as **"Obamacare"**) into law.

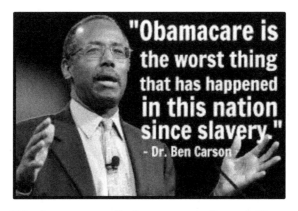

"The boost evangelical voters gave Seventh-Day Adventist Ben Carson in the polls [during the election] … is evidence of what experts are calling a continued evangelical shift away from identity politics."

documented in this book, there are still those who refuse to see him beyond being black or will credit him for many accomplishments, in particular, the efforts he made to bring unity to our Nation.

When President Obama was elected President, I was told that on the night of his inauguration, the Speaker of the House, John Boehner, Senators Paul Ryan, Mitch McConnell and other major Republicans leaders met and agreed that they would vote against anything that Obama brings to the House and the Senate. Republican leaders told President Obama to his face that he had no business being in the White House, and conservative radio personalities such as Rush Limbaugh said, "I want him to fail."

To further validate the issue of Republican opposition to President Obama's initiatives and actions, one only need recall what happened when he nominated Judge Merrick Garland to fill the vacant seat of the late Supreme Court Justice, Antonin Scalia. Conservative congressional leaders in the Republican Party said, "Delay, delay, delay." President Obama was constitutionally correct in nominating Judge Garland; however due to stalling tactics by his opponents, that is as far as it went.

At press time, some of the following facts had changed: Jeff Sessions was fired by President Donald Trump and Democrats are now the majority in the House of Representatives. We witnessed the power of the ballot in the House and Senate when the Republicans were a majority in both Houses.

Look at what has happened with Senator Jeff Sessions, a known racist from Alabama. Trump nominated him as the Attorney General, the highest legal office in our judicial system.

When Donald Trump got involved in politics and ran for President of the United States in 2016, he was determined to detonate the legitimacy of Barack Obama's presidency. This,

Time **Magazine**
President   Obama   nominates   Merrick
Garland for the Supreme Court.

**Speaker of the House, Nancy Pelosi, meeting with
President-elect Barack Obama,** Office of Speaker of
the House Nancy Pelosi, 2009. Remember that the
conservatives, because they had the majority in the
Senate and House were determined to vote against
anything and everything that Barack Obama brought
before them. I will never forget the prayers of our fore-
parents, who were slaves that one day freedom would
be favorable to us as a people. He was God-sent!

despite the fact that President Obama pulled our troops out of Afghanistan, saved the automotive and banking industries, and during his tenure, U.S. forces apprehended and killed Osama Bin Laden, a major nemesis on the U.S. war on terrorism.

Additionally, unemployment under the Obama administration was less than 5%. However, that was not the case in the black community where unemployment has always been higher than the national average.

Donald Trump engages in hyperbole with disingenuous substance covered with egregious words. His conservative policies have affected the future of the Supreme Court and Judicial system for decades to come, particularly, with his selection of two conservative nominees: Neil Gorsuch and the more contentious battle and confirmation of Brett Kavanagh. He has habitually made oxymoronic statements inconsistent with what he believes. I strongly feel that Donald Trump just might be a Manchurian President!

John Lewis was right in saying, "Trump is not a legitimate president." He wants to repeal the Affordable Health Care Act, which will affect over twenty million people who did not have coverage before, as well as the immigration law and any executive laws signed by President Barack Obama.

Achievements of the past related to Civil Rights are a cause for celebration, pride and gratitude. However, we live in a time of racial derision and are confronted and greatly challenged with many forms of discrimination which are rising across the globe under the Trump Administration, which has allegedly heightened racial division and been a lightning rod for the uptick in the number of hate groups in America.

To reverse our course and head in the right direction, someone has to step up and set about a new direction. We must organize to exact true and sustaining change. The future for black people is not only in us but "on" us, because the political

Neil Gorsuch and Brett Kavanaugh, respectively, nominated by President Trump in 2017 and 2018, respectively, and confirmed by the Republican-led U.S. Senate.

"Trump is not a legitimate president," according to U.S. Congressional Representative John Lewis from Georgia.
He wants to repeal the Affordable Health Care Act, which will affect over twenty million people who did not have coverage before, as well as the immigration law and any executive laws signed by President Barack Obama.

climate of our country and problems within our own community warrant our involvement. As I mentioned before, electing a black president was a good start to inclusion, but it was not enough. We have to stand as one nation, undivided, to stamp out hatred in every place where it exists, whether it be in minds, hearts, homes or the White House!

Danville Today: Did We Overcome? Fifty Plus Years in the Making 1963-2018

In 1963, the population of Danville was 46,577, and out of that number; there were 11,558 black people, or 24% of the population. Today, there are 43,055 people in Danville, 48% are black and 47% are white. The truth of the matter is, that Danville was larger, (population) 54 years ago than it is now, which also speaks to our growth. Today the population in Pittsylvania County is 62,426. The largest employer in Danville, Dan Rivers Mills is no longer in existence and Danville has moved from a mostly agrarian community to become more industrialized.

I have written about how things were in Danville, Virginia in 1963 when it was segregated. What I have shared are experiences that I lived. Although there has been some significant progress made from 1963-2018 and Danville has come a long way toward improving race relations, we still have a long way to go for complete healing and harmony. More than fifty years have passed since 1963, and we are still in the process of overcoming.

Unfortunately, we cannot confidently or assuredly say the words from the venerable anthem of the Civil Rights Movement, which epitomizes our struggle for equal treatment under the law because that day when "we shall overcome" has

Danville City Council Member Larry Campbell, with his wife, Elaine, and grandson, Bryce, after the elections in May 2016. This is my oldest son, Larry, who at this writing, has been elected three consecutive times to the Danville City Council. He is a dedicated, conscientious person, who cares about the welfare of our city. His mother, the family and I are very proud of him. I thank God for his wife, Elaine, my grandchildren and great grandchildren.

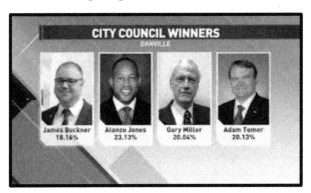

Danville City Council Election results, May 2018

Alonzo Jones is now our mayor. In every council manic election, there should always be someone from the black community running for office. When I see that, I know that my work in civil rights was not in vain. I long for the day when I can see every black person who is eligible to vote exercise that right.

yet to arrive. It was and still is our goal to abundantly proclaim that we have indeed overcome!

Our goals for Danville and our country have not dissipated through the years. Electing a black man as President was certainly phenomenal, as were the challenges we faced during the struggle for Civil Rights in 1963. Currently we can look at what progress we have made in our fight against discrimination, racism and segregation. Listed are areas in the Municipality and the business community where our demands in 1963 were made and that we enjoy today. Remember, before 1963, black people were not represented in any of these areas:

Now, there are seven members on the Danville School Board. Four are black and the superintendent is black. I served on the School Board for twelve years.

Until recently, my youngest son, Philip, was a member of the Board.

Now, the deputy to the City Manager is black.

Now, the chairperson of the Danville Housing Authority is black.

Now, there are nine members on City Council. Three are black, and the mayor, Alonzo Jones, is black. My oldest son, Larry, is on City Council.

Now, the head of Maintenance for Danville Public Schools is black.

Now, the head of the Department of Social Services is black.

Now, the Superintendent of our public-school system is black.

Now, since 1963 we have had three black mayors who served with distinction: Charles Harris, Ruby Archie and Sherman Saunders. Our current mayor is Alonzo Jones.

Racism in Danville

In 1993, I bought some property to build my house where I live today. The company told me that I would have to build within two years, or the company would buy it back. I was told that I could not sell it. Less than two weeks after the purchase, the same man came back and told me that someone wanted to buy the property and would give me ten thousand dollars more than I paid. I said to him, "I thought you said I could not sell it?" You see, the area is majority white, and they did not want me there.

After I built the house, one night, my wife and I heard some noise at the front door. When I opened the door, eggs were thrown against it and the house. 1963—1993—thirty years later, racism was still alive. I have not seen any more eggs. I pray that the community has changed!

Lawrence G. Campbell, Sr.

Integrated Danville Police Department, 2018

It gives me a great sense of appreciation and thankfulness to God that the Danville Police department is integrated. When I think about my wife on the night of June 10, when 49 other people could pray for the demonstrators who were in jail. When the chief of police told them to disperse, Rev. McGhee told them, "Let us pray." While they were praying, Chief of Police, Eugene McCain said, "Let them have it," and he beat my wife. The officers beat the demonstrators.

Now, SOVAH Health (formerly Memorial Hospital) is integrated and on the Board, there are two black members and one of the black members is my oldest son, Larry.

Now, for the first time in the history of Danville our city treasurer is a black woman, Sheila Branch.

Now, we have a black judge who presides over the Domestic Court, Judge Dale Wiley.

Now, the doors of public accommodations are open to all people regardless of race.

Now, when the garbage is collected the driving staff is integrated.

Now, the City Sheriff Department is integrated, and there are black officers.

Now, our local newspaper, *The Danville Register and Bee*, has integrated its staff with several black news reporters over the years.

Now, it is a common sight to see blacks employed in every area of our municipality and business community.

Now, the Danville Fire Department is integrated.

Now, the Danville Police Department is integrated, and the Chief's deputy is black, and about 12% of the officers are black.

Now, the Danville Public Library is integrated; and the tables and chairs have been put back so the races can now sit and read together.

Now, Danville is totally integrated, and blacks are very much a part of its growth. That does not mean that we have overcome. What we have achieved are but increments to a day when all forms of racism and bigotry will be no more. Danville is still a city that has two communities, one white and one black.

I cannot justifiably say that Danville is worse today than it was in 1963, because some progress has been made as it relates

Danville's first black firefighter, Frank Ferguson, retires after 41 years. Thank God that our fire department is now integrated, and our Fire Marshall is now a black woman!

Children at Danville public library
Do not take this picture for granted, because there was a time when black folk were admitted in the public library only to clean it and knew they could not sit down to read a book. This picture speaks to generations to come.

to race relations and equal employment opportunities. However, the major problem is still racism and the swastikas that show up every now and then. With all that we have invested in gaining our civil rights, the black community is confronted with black-on- black crime. This is most disturbing to all of us because we never thought of a day when we would become our own worst enemy.

During 2016 in our city, there were 16 murders, in which all killed were black, and all those who committed the murders were black, except one. This was the highest number of homicides ever in the history of Danville. Recently, when a white doctor was shot in our city, allegedly by a black man, the white community became alarmed and offered a reward. However, as long as the violence remained in the black community, there was barely a ripple or sound of concern from the white community.

A similar thing happened related to the selling of drugs. Some wanted drugs sold only in the black community. America did not care if blacks were drug addicts, but when drugs spilled over into the white community, America became involved in defeating the selling of heroin and other forms of drugs.

When blacks are killed, we call it a "March." In the white community, when whites are harmed, they call it a "Walk." Regardless of what we call it, violence or drug addiction knows no race or boundaries. Already this year, there have been two homicides. We all live in the same house and it is called the City of Danville.

In regard to the White Church, there is a divide that has yet to be bridged. Not only in Danville, but throughout this country black people have been joining white congregations, but for the most part, white people do not join black churches. In most instances, when you see white people in the black congregation, they are white women, married to or dating a

Confederate Flag rally in Danville, VA, 2015.
All over Danville, it is not unusual to see large, Confederate flags, flying. When you enter Danville, you see the symbols of white supremacy.

White nationalist "Unite the Right" rally in Charlottesville, VA, on August 12, 2017. Vehicle that killed Heather Heyer and injured 19 others. It was agonizing for me to have seen the racial hatred, expressed in such a demonic display in Charlottesville, Virginia. The loss of life that was so unnecessary, all because of racial bigotry, to have seen President Donald Trump downplaying the seriousness of this tragedy is disgusting.

black man. White men, their children and wives are not seen as members of a black church.

Also, when black people join a white congregation, more often than not, the white people leave and go to another church and that church becomes a black majority. I see it as blatant racism, particularly when the white pulpit is silent on the Confederate flag and violence in the black community, but they will talk about violence in Afghanistan.

Not a word is uttered on "Black Lives Matter," the KKK or racial profiling. Therefore, the black preacher is still a voice in the city for justice and fairness for all people. The voice for righteousness and justice must not be put under a bushel but spoken from all of the 400 pulpits in the city.

If the White Church would speak out against the KKK, Neo-Nazis and the Confederate Flag publicly, on Sunday morning, that's when the word will become flesh. That cannot just happen behind stain glass windows. Our convictions on race must not be isolated to Sunday morning, but must be a voice heard in the wilderness of our community. Why is it that you do not hear any white preacher in our city speak out publicly against racial issues?

In response to some of the issues in Danville, I have taken an active role in coalition building. In 2013, I went before City Council and asked that they appoint a Race Relations Committee, for which they were very receptive. However, the committee was discontinued. I often wondered why, and I asked what happened, but no clear explanation was given.

A few years later, in 2015, I started the Community and Law Enforcement Partnership Day to create a relationship between the two groups, particularly the black community. I held meetings in the community, and I engaged with the White Church, where one of ministers said if the Community Day were held in a central location, such as Ballou Park, then whites

"**I chose to organize in 2015 the Law-Eforcement Community Day** – the purpose of which was to bring about a better relationship between our police department and the black community.

Bishop Lawrence G. Campbell Sr., a local civil rights leader and pastor and co-founder at Bibleway Cathedral, received a first-of-its-kind award from Averett University.

would come. In other words, they were not comfortable in the black community, which was on Grant Street where our church is located.

Despite all that we have gone through, there are still those in the white community who are very amenable to working together to create a better environment that will improve race relations. Such a group is the Womack Foundation, named after my good friend, Charles Womack, who assured the truth about Danville would be revealed. The organization has done a remarkable job as a support group across the racial divide.

Therefore, I say for the advances, and for the road ahead: God bless Danville, city that I love, stand beside her and guide her through the night with a light from above. From the east side, to the west side, from the north side, to the south side, God bless Danville, my home sweet home.

Martin Luther King Jr. *I Have a Dream*, **1963.** I shall never forget the March on Washington, and to hear my friend, Dr. Martin Luther King, deliver the message of all time, "I Have a Dream." It was just five years later that he was assassinated.

September 15, 1963, 16th Street Baptist Church in Birmingham, Alabama

"YOU CAN KILL A MAN, BUT YOU CAN'T KILL AN IDEA."
Medgar Evers

Medgar Evers, assassinated by Byron De La Beckwith of Greenwood, Mississippi. on June 12, 1963. 1963 was indeed the "long hot summer." We lost, in death, a great civil rights fighter-Medgar Evers, by an assassin's bullet. We saw four innocent black girls killed in the 16th Street Baptist Church in Birmingham, Alabama, bombed by the KKK.

Clockwise from center, Gloria Campbell, Apostle Lawrence G. Campbell, Sr., daughter Allethia, daughter Angela, son Philip, daughter Hope and son Lawrence, Jr.

Bishop Lawrence G. Campbell, Sr. and Gloria Campbell, with children, grandchildren and great grandchildren.

About the Author

Lawrence G. Campbell Sr. was born in Danville, Virginia, and served honorably in the United States Navy. He played an integral role in Danville's fight for Civil Rights as a vocal leader, who has worked stridently to bring the community of Danville together in an effort to create racial harmony and healing.

In 1953, he and his wife, Mrs. Gloria Campbell, started the Bible Way Church. In 1988, he was appointed to the Danville School board, and became the first black chairman of the school board. In 1991, he was consecrated Apostle by the board of Bishops.

Currently, he is the Senior Chief Apostle of the International Bible Way Church of Jesus Christ Inc. and serves on the Executive Board of Bishops. He is the Diocesan of the Virginia State Diocese.

In 2017, Apostle Campbell authored a story titled, *A Life of Divinity and Alleviating the Racial Divide*, that was included in the anthology, *Our Black Fathers--Brave, Bold and Beautiful!*

Most recently, the father of five successful children: Allethia, Lawrence Jr., Angela, Philip and Hope, became the first recipient of Averett University's President's Service Award during Founder's Day in January 2019.

The award is given in recognition for "exemplary service to the community and university," where he received a B.A. in Psychology. Apostle Campbell also holds an A.A. from Virginia Seminary and College in Lynchburg, Virginia, a master's degree from A&T State University in Greensboro, North Carolina and a Doctor of Divinity from Virginia University, Lynchburg.

Apostle Campbell and Mrs. Campbell at the home of President Tiffany Franks of Averett University, for reception prior to giving of the award.

Apostle Campbell receiving the award

Apostle Campbell, President Franks presenting flowers to Mrs. Campbell

WKBY 1080 radio station also streaming at WKBY 1080.net 24/7. This inspiration station features Apostle Lawrence G. Campbell, Sr. Practical living broadcast Monday through Friday at 7:30 a.m. and 3:30 p.m.

Chatham, Virginia – WKBY Radio Station speaks to the current issues of the day.

Acknowledgements

Anita Royston, Five Sisters Publishing
Publisher, Editor

Joslyn Gaines Vanderpool
Chief Editor, Co-Creator, Brave Bold Beautiful Books

Marcus McGee, Pegasus Book, Parnassus Press
Associate Publisher, Associate Editor

Felecia M
Book Cover Concept, *1963 A Turning Point in Civil Rights*

Jeremiah Johnson, Johnson Enterprises
Final Cover Design, *1963 A Turning Point in Civil Rights*